The Countries

Turkey

Kristin Van Cleaf
ABDO Publishing Company

visit us at
www.abdopublishing.com

Published by ABDO Publishing Company, 8000 West 78th Street, Edina, Minnesota 55439.
Copyright © 2008 by Abdo Consulting Group, Inc. International copyrights reserved in all
countries. No part of this book may be reproduced in any form without written permission from the
publisher. The Checkerboard Library™ is a trademark and logo of ABDO Publishing Company.

Printed in the United States.

Interior Photos: Alamy pp. 5, 9, 10, 25, 31; AP Images pp. 13, 32; Corbis pp. 19, 34; Getty Images
    p. 21; Heidi M.D. Elston pp. 6, 22, 26, 36; iStockPhoto p. 25; Peter Arnold pp. 29, 37

Editors: Megan M. Gunderson, BreAnn Rumsch
Art Direction & Maps: Neil Klinepier

Library of Congress Cataloging-in-Publication Data

Van Cleaf, Kristin, 1976-
    Turkey / Kristin Van Cleaf.
        p. cm. -- (The countries)
    Includes index.
    ISBN 978-1-59928-787-4
    1. Turkey--Juvenile literature. 2. Turkey--History--Juvenile literature. 3. Turkey--Politics and
government--Juvenile literature.
4. Turkey--Civilization--Juvenile literature. I. Title.
    DR417.4.V36 2007
    956.1--dc22
                                        2007010184

Contents

Merhaba!

Hello from Turkey! This nation lies in both Asia and Europe, between the Black and Mediterranean seas. The Asian part of Turkey is called Asia Minor, or Anatolia. The European section is an area called Thrace. Turkey is a country of many mountains and even some volcanoes. Earthquakes are also common.

Turkey was once part of the great Ottoman Empire. In fact, the country's largest city has been the capital of several empires. Now called İstanbul (ihs-TAHN-bool), this historic city was once known as Constantinople. It is the only major city in the world that lies on both the European and Asian continents.

Turkish **culture** has endured throughout the area's long history. And, Islam has also remained an important part of the people's lives. From kebabs to evil eye charms, tradition is important in the current nation.

Timeline

2000 BC	Hittites arrive in present-day Turkey
546 BC	Persians invade the region
334 BC	Alexander the Great and the Macedonians defeat the Persians
AD 330	Roman emperor Constantine I moves his capital to Constantinople
395	The eastern half of the Roman Empire becomes the Byzantine Empire
1071	Byzantine emperor Romanus IV Diogenes attacks the Seljuk Empire and loses
1453	The Ottomans conquer Constantinople and rename it İstanbul; the Byzantine Empire ends
1839	The Tanzimat reforms end laws that governed people differently based on religion
1914	The Ottoman Empire enters World War I
1920	Sultan Mehmed VI signs the Treaty of Sèvres, leaving just İstanbul and parts of Anatolia to the Ottomans
1923	The Treaty of Lausanne determines the country's current borders; Kemal Atatürk becomes president of the new Republic of Turkey
2005	The European Union begins discussing membership with Turkey

Empire to Republic

The history of Turkey's people is much older than the country itself. People have lived in the region since at least 8000 BC. Around 2000 BC, Hittites arrived from Europe or central Asia. They settled central Anatolia, conquered the surrounding lands, and created a great empire.

Around 1200 BC, various groups began dividing up large areas of Anatolia. Persians invaded in 546 BC. Then in 334 BC, Alexander the Great and the Macedonians defeated the Persians.

Next, Anatolia fell under the control of the Roman Empire. In AD 330, Emperor Constantine I made Byzantium a new capital of the Roman Empire. It then became known as Constantinople, the city of Constantine. In 395, the Roman Empire split in half. The east side became known as the Byzantine Empire.

Islamic Oguz Turkish tribes began conquering land neighboring Anatolia in the middle 900s. In 1037, they founded the Seljuk Empire. Byzantine emperor Romanus IV Diogenes attacked the Seljuks in 1071, but the Seljuks won.

After this, many Turkish tribes slowly began moving to the region. Islam and the Turkish language slowly replaced Christianity and the Greek language of Anatolia.

Then in 1243, Asian Mongols conquered the Seljuk Empire. Turkish tribes fought back, and a group now called the Ottomans took control. They continued west to fight the Byzantines. In 1453, the Ottomans conquered Constantinople. The city became the growing Ottoman Empire's capital, İstanbul. Its capture ended the Byzantine Empire.

Constantine I was also known as "Constantine the Great." He ruled the Roman Empire until AD *337.*

The Ottoman Empire was strongest during the 1500s. One of its greatest leaders, Sultan Süleyman (soo-lay-MAHN) I, accomplished many military victories. In 1526, his army captured most of Hungary in the Battle of Mohács. Sultan Süleyman expanded the empire's borders west to Morocco, south to Yemen, and east to Persia.

Sultan Süleyman I at the Battle of Mohács

After Sultan Süleyman's death in 1566, the empire began to lose much of its territory. By the early 1800s, several nations under Ottoman rule had started demanding independence.

Throughout the 1800s, war with Russia was common. Russia gradually took Ottoman land along the Black Sea. In the 1850s, Great Britain and France helped defeat the Russians during the **Crimean** (kreye-MEE-uhn) **War**. But Russia regained some of its lost land through war from 1877 to 1878.

Meanwhile, Ottoman rulers tried to reform the government to stop the empire's **decline**. Beginning in 1839, the Tanzimat reforms officially ended laws that governed people differently based on their religion. In 1876, a new **constitution** created a representative government with a **parliament**.

However, Ottoman sultan Abdülhamid (ahb-dool-hah-MEED) II set aside the constitution. Under Sultan Abdülhamid's rule, Islam again became the favored religion. And between 1894 and 1896, he violently destroyed Armenian Christians in the empire.

During the late 1890s, small groups of students and military officers opposed the sultan's harsh rule. They became known as the Young Turks. In 1906, they created the Committee of Union and Progress. And in 1908, they convinced Sultan Abdülhamid to create a new constitution and parliament.

Despite efforts by the Young Turks to regain lost territory, the empire continued to shrink. By 1914, Thrace was its only European land. That year, the empire entered **World War I**.

After losing the war, military hero Mustafa Kemal created a temporary government. The new Turkish Grand National Assembly elected him president in 1920. Later that year, Sultan Mehmed VI signed the unpopular Treaty of Sèvres. It broke up the empire, which retained only İstanbul and parts of Anatolia.

In 1923, Mustafa Kemal's government signed the Treaty of Lausanne. This determined the country's current borders. And on October 29, the Grand National Assembly declared Mustafa Kemal president of the new Republic of Turkey.

The new government made many changes to society. Islam was no longer the nation's official religion. Women gained the right to vote and hold public office. The Turkish language was reformed, and everyone adopted last names. The assembly named Mustafa Kemal *Atatürk*, or "Father of Turks."

In 1950, Turkey's Democratic Party gained control of the government and began new reforms. Their changes caused a large national **debt** and limited freedom of speech. So, a new **constitution** and prime minister were put in place in 1961.

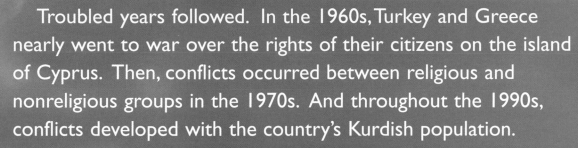

Troubled years followed. In the 1960s, Turkey and Greece nearly went to war over the rights of their citizens on the island of Cyprus. Then, conflicts occurred between religious and nonreligious groups in the 1970s. And throughout the 1990s, conflicts developed with the country's Kurdish population.

In 1999, Turkey began reforms to join the **European Union (EU)**. These included more rights for both Kurds and women. In 2005, the EU began discussing membership with Turkey.

Turkey must continue its human rights and equality reforms to be considered for EU membership.

Surrounded by Seas

Turkey lies at a place where Asia and Europe meet. It is also close to Africa. And, Turkey borders large bodies of water. The Black Sea is to the north, the Mediterranean Sea lies south, and the Aegean (ee-JEE-uhn) Sea is to the west. The Sea of Marmara connects these seas in the northwest. It lies between two straits, the Bosporus and the Dardanelles.

Turkey is slightly larger than the state of Texas. Bulgaria and Greece border its northwestern tip. Its eastern neighbors are Georgia, Armenia, Azerbaijan, and Iran. Iraq and Syria lie to the southeast.

Much of Turkey is mountainous. Rivers such as the Sakarya and the Kızıl Irmak (keh-ZEHL eer-mahk) begin south of the northern mountain ranges. They flow north through rocky gorges into the Black Sea. The Pontic Mountains are in the northeast along the narrow Black Sea coast.

In the west, many villages lie in the valleys of the Gediz, Büyük Menderes, and Küçük Menderes rivers. Numerous small islands lie off the western coast in the Aegean Sea.

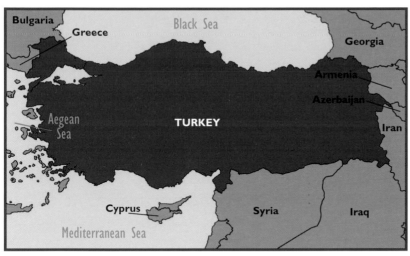

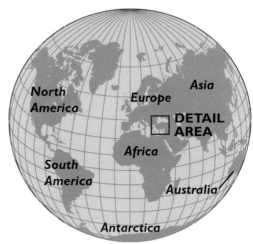

Along the narrow Mediterranean coast are the Antalya and Adana lowland plains. The high, steep cliffs of the Taurus Mountains begin west of Antalya. Waterfalls pour from these high areas, which extend throughout the south.

The Anatolian **Plateau** is an area of river valleys and high plateaus in central Turkey. It also holds the shallow, salty Tuz Lake.

The eastern Anatolian Plateau contains Turkey's largest lake, Lake Van, and many ancient volcanoes. An inactive volcano named Mount Ararat is Turkey's highest peak at 16,949 feet (5,166 m). The Tigris and Euphrates rivers flow through southeastern Turkey on their way to Syria, Iraq, and the Persian Gulf.

The seas and the mountains affect Turkey's climate. Overall it is dry, especially during the hot summers. The central areas are drier than the high peaks. Snow lasts longest in the mountains.

Coastal regions have mild winters. But, inland temperatures often fall below 32 degrees Fahrenheit (0°C). In the west, it can reach as low as -4 degrees Fahrenheit (-20°C). In the east, people sometimes bundle up for -40 degrees Fahrenheit (-40°C)!

Rainfall

AVERAGE YEARLY RAINFALL

Inches		_Centimeters_
Under 20		Under 50
20–40		50–100
40–60		100–150
Over 60		Over 150

Temperature

AVERAGE TEMPERATURE

Fahrenheit		_Celsius_
Over 65°		Over 18°
54°–65°		12°–18°
43°–54°		6°–12°
32°–43°		0°–6°
21°–32°		-6°–0°
Below 21°		Below -6°

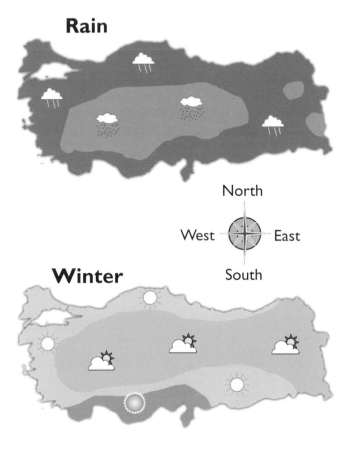

Rain

North
West — East
South

Winter

Summer

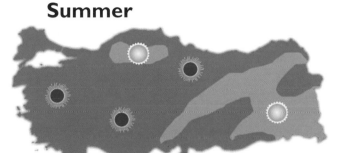

Wildlife

Turkey's land contains many varieties of plant and animal life. **Steppe** grasslands are common in central Anatolia and its eastern valleys and **basins**. There are also grasslands in the southeast and in the lowlands of Thrace.

Forests cover the rest of the country. The Pontic forest lies on the eastern Black Sea coast. There, many alder, sweet chestnut, and oriental spruce trees grow. Common shrubs include laurel, holly, walnut, and myrtle.

Deciduous (dih-SIH-juh-wuhs) forests cover other areas along the Black Sea. Beech, fir, yew, oak, and hornbeam trees grow in these woods. Coniferous trees are common above 3,300 feet (1,000 m). And, many alpine grasses grow at twice this altitude.

Oak, juniper, fir, and pine trees are common in the drier interior lands. These trees, as well as cedar, maple, and beech, also grow in the southern mountains. Myrtle, wild olive, carob, and cypress grow near the Aegean and Mediterranean seas.

Wild animals such as wolves, wildcats, jackals, and hyenas are common in Turkey's forests. These woods are also home to bears, deers, mountain goats, gazelles, and boars. As for birds, there are many quails, partridges, wild geese, and bustards. **Domesticated** animals such as water buffalo, Angora goats, and camels also live in Turkey.

Camels are common in southwest Turkey.

Turks

Most of the people who live in Turkey are Turks. Kurds make up the largest **minority**, and many live in the mountainous southeast. A few descendants of people from the Caucasus Mountains live near the Black Sea. Some Arabs, Greeks, Jews, and Armenians also live in Turkey.

Turkish is the official language. The Ottomans used a similar language, but the Turkish government changed the alphabet in 1928. This made the language easier to learn and write. In addition to Turkish, many minorities also speak their own languages, such as Kurdish, Arabic, or Armenian.

Almost all Turks are **Muslims**. Still, the nation's **constitution** allows religious freedom. So, small numbers of Jews and Christians also live in Turkey.

Turkish homes vary throughout the country. Near the Black Sea, many people live in thatch-roofed timber cottages. In Anatolia, homes are often made of sun-dried brick with flat roofs. Some homes have two floors, with the family's animals

living on the lower level. In cities, apartments are common. Family is important, and extended families may live together.

When Turkish children turn six, they begin school for five years. About half of these students go on to three-year middle schools. Then, students may attend high school or technical or **vocational** school. Many students who finish secondary school go on to higher education. Two of Turkey's largest universities are in İstanbul and Ankara (AHNG-kuh-ruh).

Turks often wear modern, Western-style clothing. However, some still wear traditional Islamic garments. Men may wear a loose cloak and baggy pants. Women may wear a simple blouse and pantaloons. Some women also cover their heads, and sometimes lower face, with a scarf.

Turkish food is rich in variety. Basics include breads, such as white bread called *ekmek* and flat bread called *pide* (pee-DEH). Eggplant or zucchini cooked in butter with tomatoes, green peppers, and onions are popular dishes.

A common meat preparation in Turkey is the kebab. **Skewered** vegetables and cubes of meat make a shish kebab.

Döner (der-NEHR) kebabs are skewered stacks of lamb and other meats. *Köfte* (kerf-TEH) are patties or balls of meat that can be grilled or eaten raw.

Fresh seasonal fruits make the sweetest desserts. Puddings and layered pastries are other favorites. Baklava is a sweet pastry often eaten with thick Turkish coffee. Many Turks drink tea all day long.

İstanbul's Spice Bazaar offers spices, honey, dried fruits, nuts, and other delicious treats.

Stuffed Figs

- 12 dried figs
- 1 cup hazelnuts, chopped
- 8 tablespoons heavy whipping cream
- 1 1/2 cups water
- 1/3 cup sugar

Combine hazelnuts and sugar. Remove the stems from the figs, and use a teaspoon to make holes in the centers of the figs. Fill the figs with the nut mixture. Place the stuffed figs in a shallow frying pan, nut mixture sides up. Add water to the pan, cover, and simmer for 30 minutes. Remove from heat and allow to cool. Whip the cream. Serve figs cold with whipped cream and enjoy!

AN IMPORTANT NOTE TO THE CHEF: Always have an adult help with the preparation and cooking of food. Never use kitchen utensils or appliances without adult permission and supervision.

LANGUAGE

English	Turkish
Hello	Merhaba (MEHR-hah-bah)
Good-bye	Hoşçakal (hohsh-CHAH-kahl)
Yes	Evet (eh-VEHT)
No	Hayır (HAH-yuhr)
Please	Lütfen (LOOT-fehn)
Thank you	Teşekkür ederim (teh-shehk-KOOR eh-DEH-reem)
You're welcome	Birşey değil (beer-SHAY deh-EEL)

Agriculture and Tourism

Turkey has a mixed **economy**. In the past, agriculture was strongest. Today, industry and services such as tourism are most important.

About half of Turks work in agriculture. Most farms lie near the coasts, where land is fertile. Farmers grow grains, such as wheat, barley, rye, corn, and rice. Farms also produce apples, grapes, oranges, figs, and olives. And, farmers raise cattle, sheep, goats, and water buffalo.

Turkey's land holds a variety of natural resources, including iron ore, copper, mercury, and gold. It also has large amounts of coal. And, Turkey is developing hydroelectric power plants on rivers such as the Sakarya and the Kızıl Irmak.

Many Turks also work in manufacturing. They commonly make **textiles**, chemicals, and foods. Steel and sugar made from sugar beets are other major products.

Turkey trades with countries such as France, Italy, Russia, the United Kingdom, and the United States. But Germany is its main trade partner. Turkey exports iron, textiles, manufactured items, nuts, fruits, and vegetables. The country imports petroleum, chemicals, and motor vehicles.

Tourism is a strong part of Turkey's **economy**. Millions of tourists from all over the world visit the country's cities and seacoasts. Popular sights include ancient Troy, Pamukkale, and the **unique** rock formations in Cappadocia.

Swimming in Pamukkale's hot springs is no longer allowed. But, tourists still love visiting these amazing calcium formations.

Turkey is a leading producer of grapes, including those dried to make raisins.

Historic Cities

İstanbul was once the capital of the Byzantine and Ottoman empires. Today, it is Turkey's largest city. Because it lies on the Bosporus, its shipping port is vital to trade. İstanbul is also an **economic** and **cultural** center.

İstanbul has more than 1,000 beautiful mosques. Two of the most famous are the Mosque of Süleyman and the

Because of its beautiful tile work, the Mosque of Ahmed I is more commonly know as the Blue Mosque.

blue-tiled Mosque of Ahmed I. İstanbul also boasts the grand Topkapı Palace, which was once the home of Turkish sultans. Ruins of ancient **aqueducts** still stand. And, the city's covered bazaar has more than 4,000 shops.

Turkey's capital and second-largest city, Ankara, sits at the base of a mountain. It is home to many universities and is an **economic** center. Many local people go to Ankara to sell wool from the region's famous long-haired Angora goats.

Ankara also has historic buildings, such as the Roman Temple of Roma and Augustus. The ancient, square Alâeddin Mosque is also in Ankara. And, the modern city is known for its large Atatürk **Mausoleum**.

İzmir (ihz-MIHR), once called Smyrna, lies along the Aegean coast. It is Turkey's third-largest city and one of the country's largest ports. Figs, cotton, olive oil, silks, and carpets are exported from İzmir. And, it is one of the headquarters for **NATO**.

İzmir is one of the oldest Mediterranean cities. One of its important landmarks, the ancient **agora**, is still being uncovered. Today, İzmir is in a highly populated region. Tourism is a growing part of the city's economy.

Travel and Talk

In Turkey, people and goods travel using a variety of methods. Most people use public transportation, such as buses. Or, they ride in shared taxis called *dolmuşes*. Railcars run between large cities, but they are often delayed.

The road system has grown and become more important in recent years. However, only about one in 15 people owns a car. Much freight is moved by truck.

The Black and Mediterranean seas are important for shipping goods. Turkey has main ports at İstanbul, İskenderun, İzmir, and Mersin. Above the land and the seas, air travel is possible through numerous airports. İstanbul, Ankara, and İzmir offer both domestic and international flights.

When people can't be together, they still have several ways to communicate. Most families have home telephones, but cellular telephones are growing in popularity. Service is best in cities. Members of the upper class often own computers, too. More than 16 million Turks use the Internet.

Two bridges stretch across the Bosporus. This strait has been important for trade and shipping for hundreds of years.

Turks generally have freedom of the press. *Milliyet*, *Sabah*, and *Hürriyet* are the country's main newspapers. Kurdish speakers often read *Azadi* and *Welat*. Many people also own televisions. The Turkish Radio-Television Corporation runs several radio and television networks. There are also many private stations.

Governing Turkey

Turkey's government is a **parliamentary democracy**. The current **constitution** was approved in 1982. It protects government organizations from criticism and attacks by Turks. But, it does not give complete freedom of speech to its citizens.

The Grand National Assembly is Turkey's legislative branch. Voters elect its 550 members to five-year terms. The assembly makes laws, approves treaties, and can declare war.

Turkey's president and prime minister share executive power. The Grand National Assembly elects the president to a seven-year term. The president has the power to send laws back to the assembly to be reworked. He or she may also suggest changes to the constitution or dissolve the assembly.

The president selects an assembly member as prime minister. This person carries out government policies and works closely with the cabinet, or Council of Ministers. These ministers oversee various government departments.

Turkey's judicial branch has courts throughout the country. The Constitutional Court decides whether laws passed by the assembly are legal. Lower courts hear criminal trials and cases regarding business and family conflicts. Appeals courts review these decisions.

For local government, the president approves a governor for each of Turkey's 81 **provinces**. The people vote for council members. In villages, people elect a headman and a council of elders.

All Turkish citizens who are at least 18 years old may vote. The Grand National Assembly meets in the capital city, Ankara.

Celebrating Tradition

In Turkey, holidays honor important days throughout the year. Many people begin the year by celebrating New Year's Eve. On this night, people enjoy a special dinner and spend time with their families and friends.

On April 23, Turks have a **unique** holiday called National Sovereignty and Children's Day. It celebrates the founding of

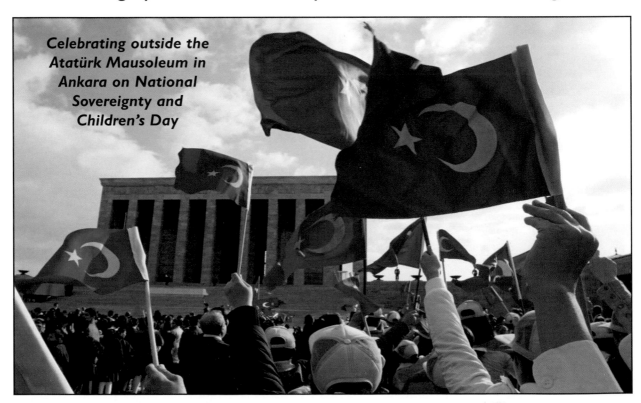

Celebrating outside the Atatürk Mausoleum in Ankara on National Sovereignty and Children's Day

the nation and the children who will grow up to run it. On this day, children take the place of government officials! Many sign laws dealing with education and the **environment**.

An important **Muslim** holiday is Ramadan. It honors when the prophet Muhammad first received **revelations** of the Koran. For an entire month, Muslims go without food from sunrise to sunset. At the end, they celebrate by eating sweet treats during three days called *Şeker Bayramı* (sheh-KEHR beye-rah-MUH), or Sugar Holiday.

Another Muslim holiday is *Kurban* (koor-BAHN) *Bayramı*, or Sacrifice Holiday. During this time, many Muslims make **pilgrimages** to Mecca, a Muslim holy city in Saudi Arabia. And, people sometimes sacrifice an animal to give meat to the poor.

October 29 is Republic Day. It honors the day Turkey was declared a nation in 1923. Turks also honor the death of national hero Kemal Atatürk, the republic's first president. He died at 9:05 AM on November 10, 1938. At this time every year, Atatürk is remembered with a moment of silence.

Arts and Architecture

Turks often attend soccer matches or kick around soccer balls in the street.

Turkish **culture** is a rich mix of everyday activities and traditional arts. Turks like to attend concerts and movies. Families may go on picnics or relax by watching television. Soccer is the favorite sport of many Turks. Many people also enjoy grease wrestling, basketball, and swimming.

In urban areas, theater is popular. Turks often watch *karagöz*, a shadow play with puppets cast on a curtain. Another popular kind of theater, *orta oyunu*, is a type of comedy.

Turkish women often spend time volunteering or visiting friends. The men commonly socialize and play card games or backgammon in teahouses. Visiting a *meyhane*, a type of restaurant, for cold foods and drinks is also a tradition.

Turks have a rich arts **culture** as well. For hundreds of years, people have prized beautiful, elaborately designed Turkish carpets. Villagers still weave these lovely rugs on hand looms.

Music is also important to Turks. Twin sister pianists Güher and Süher Pekinel are highly praised by music lovers. Violinists Suna Kan and Ayla Erduran are known internationally.

Folk music varies by region, religion, and cultural group. Kurds sing to pass on traditions. Turks often play folk melodies on the *saz*, a long-necked, stringed instrument. Fiddles, drums, bagpipes, flutes, tambourines, and cymbals may accompany it. Turks dance and play music at festivals and other important events.

Architecture is one of the most celebrated Turkish arts. One of the finest examples is İstanbul's Hagia Sophia. This domed Byzantine cathedral was built in the 500s.

Many of Turkey's other great buildings were designed by Mimar Sinan in the 1500s. The word *mimar* means "the architect" in Turkish. Many people consider Sinan's Mosque of Süleyman one of the world's most beautiful mosques.

Some Turkish mosques are covered in distinctive blue **ceramic** tiles. They were painted in beautiful designs in the 1500s and 1600s. Artists from İznik created some of the most treasured pieces.

İznik tiles decorate numerous Turkish mosques.

Turkish artists also make elegant glasswork, including colorful oil lamps. A **unique** example of Turkish glasswork is the evil eye charm. Turks believe these blue and white glass beads protect against bad luck or the evil eye.

Turks have had a strong tradition of folk literature. Other writings focus on religion or life during the Ottoman Empire. Modern Turkish literature covers nationalism, social justice, and history. Minstrels called *âşiks* recite stories called *hikâye* or poetry called *siir*.

Famous Turkish writers include novelist Orhan Pamuk, who won the 2006 **Nobel Prize** for Literature. Sabahattin Ali and Sait Faik have written excellent short stories. Aziz Nesin is known for his **satire**. These writers add their names

Orhan Pamuk was the first Turkish author to win the Nobel Prize for Literature.

to the list of people who continue to promote the **unique culture** of Turkey.

Glossary

agora - a gathering place, especially an ancient Greek marketplace.

aqueduct - a type of canal or similar structure that carries water over long distances.

architecture - the art of planning and designing buildings.

basin - the entire region of land drained by a river and its tributaries.

ceramic - of or relating to a nonmetallic product, such as pottery or porcelain.

constitution - the laws that govern a country.

Crimean War - from 1853 to 1856, when Great Britain, France, and the Ottoman Empire fought against Russia over territory near the Black Sea.

culture - the customs, arts, and tools of a nation or people at a certain time.

debt - something owed to someone, usually money.

decline - to tend toward an inferior state or a weaker condition.

domesticated - animals that are used by and adapted to life with humans.

economy - the way a nation uses its money, goods, and natural resources.

environment - all the surroundings that affect the growth and well-being of a living thing.

European Union (EU) - an organization of European countries that works toward political, economic, governmental, and social unity.

mausoleum - a large, usually stone, above-ground tomb.

minority - a racial, religious, or political group that is different from the larger group of which it is a part.

Muslim - a person who follows Islam. Islam is a religion based on the teachings of the prophet Muhammad as they appear in the Koran.

NATO - North Atlantic Treaty Organization. A group formed by the United States, Canada, and some European countries in 1949. It tries to create peace among its nations and protect them from common enemies.

Nobel Prize - an award for someone who has made outstanding achievements in his or her field of study.

parliament - the highest lawmaking body of some governments.

parliamentary democracy - a form of government in which the decisions of the nation are made by the people through the elected parliament.

pilgrimage - a journey to a holy place.

plateau - a raised area of flat land.

province - a geographical or governmental division of a country.

revelation - something that is revealed by God to humans.

satire - writing that makes fun of human faults.

skewer - to use a thin piece of metal or wood to fasten meat or vegetables for roasting.

steppe - any large, flat plain without trees.

textile - a woven fabric or cloth.

unique - being the only one of its kind.

vocational - relating to training in a skill or a trade to be pursued as a career.

World War I - from 1914 to 1918, fought in Europe. Great Britain, France, Russia, the United States, and their allies were on one side. Germany, Austria-Hungary, and their allies were on the other side.

Web Sites

To learn more about Turkey, visit ABDO Publishing Company on the World Wide Web at **www.abdopublishing.com**. Web sites about Turkey are featured on our Book Links page. These links are routinely monitored and updated to provide the most current information available.

Index